More Than A CONQUEROR

I Am a Possessor!

William Campbell

Gazelle PRESS

More Than a Conqueror
by William M. Campbell, Jr.

Copyright ©2004 William M. Campbell, Jr.
All rights reserved. This book is protected under the copyright laws of the United States of America. This book may not be copied or reprinted for commercial gain or profit. The use of short quotations or occasional page copying for personal or group study is permitted and encouraged. Permission will be granted upon request. Unless otherwise identified, Scripture quotations are from the King James Version of the Bible.

ISBN 1-58169-154-8
For Worldwide Distribution
Printed in the U.S.A.

Gazelle Press
P.O. Box 191540 • Mobile, AL 36619
800-367-8203

Table of Contents

Dedication

To the most remarkable mother
of any man anywhere—Edith Campbell.
Your life teaches me never to give up.

Acknowledgments

This work began in 1996, which was a year in which God confirmed a significant change of course for my life and ministry. As I reflect on that year, my heart is filled with profound gratitude for all the pastors and congregations who opened their doors and their hearts to receive the messages contained in this work during that and subsequent years. To specifically express my gratitude, I chronicled the pastors and churches where each message was preached. I hope that this expression will not only begin to repay my debt of gratitude, but will also serve as an apology for the delay in getting the message out.

Chapter 1	12/31/96	Mt. Zion A.M.E. Church
New Brunswick NJ		Pastor Henry A. Hildebrand
Chapter 2&3	12/26-27/97	Faith Center for All Nations
Muncie, IN		Pastor Larry L. Carther
Chapter 4	2/2/03	Anderson Chapel A.M.E. Church
Killeen TX		Pastor William M. Campbell, Jr.
Chapter 5	3/15/96	Mt. Calvary Holy Church of Amer.
Milwaukee WI		Bishop Gertrude L.N. Pitts
Chapter 6/7	2/16,23/03	Anderson Chapel A.M.E. Church
Killeen TX		Pastor William M. Campbell, Jr.
Chapter 8&9	11/14-15/96	Victory Temple A.M.E. Church
Duncanville TX		Pastor Beverly Freeman
Chapter 10	11/19/00	Greater Garth Chapel A.M.E. Ch.
Dallas TX		Pastor William M. Campbell, Jr.
Chapter 11	6/6/96	Pentecostal Tabernacle COGIC
Nashville TX		Bishop Jerry L. Maynard
Chapter 12/13	12/5-6/96	Evergreen Baptist Church
Las Vegas, NV		Pastor Nathaniel Whitney
Chapter 14	6/7/96	Pentecostal Tabernacle COGIC
Nashville TX		Bishop Jerry L. Maynard

Introduction

The opening scene in the book of Joshua takes us to the base of Mt. Nebo in the mountains of Pisgah. This location is on the east side of the Jordan river. Across the river, within eyesight, is the city of Jericho and the land that the Lord promised to the children of Israel. Forty years before, they had come to this same point but failed to enter and receive their blessing. Instead, due to their unbelief, they had to turn back and wander in the wilderness for 40 years until an entire generation died out. Their great deliverer, Moses, died, and a new generation leader, Joshua, was anointed for a monumental task: to conquer and possess the land of Canaan. They were on the verge of a new season of discovery.

The Lord did not tell Joshua and the children of Israel to conquer the land, however. The Lord told them to possess the land. The word "possess" means to evict the previous tenant. For more than 400 years, someone else had been living in the Hebrews' land.

You may be like the children of Israel, on the verge of a new season of discovery—a breakthrough in your life. Maybe you are tired of the enemy of your soul living rent-free in your blessings while you wander in the wilderness. Rejoice! Your wandering days are over, too. It is time for you to conquer and possess what is rightfully yours. Be encouraged—you too are a possessor!

As in all my writings, I encourage you to first read the book of Joshua in order to get a good scriptural background. It is best to know the Bible first before reading other books about it. As you read, my prayer is that the conqueror inside of you will come alive and you will arise and possess what God has for you.

plosions or eruptions in our behavior, rev

that there are some issues in our lives

never before addressed.

How can we find new strength

these painful memories on

move past our memories

that need to happen in

must be reconciled

In the mi

wonde

po

_ we were ever born. unfortunately, the memories of hurts, pain, and loss along with the fear of having them occur once again keep many of us from accomplishing our dreams and fulfilling that destiny. Many of us are saved, but we are still hurting and angry over things that happened in the past. As a result we cannot move forward in the peace of God to do what He has told us to do.

Many Christians have declared that "There is nothing in my heart against anyone" or "I just love everybody," only to encounter someone or something that reminds us of a past hurt. This painful memory often causes ex-

ealing to us
that we have

n God by putting aside
e and for all? In order to
nd fears, there are three things
our lives: We must be healed, we
, and we must be resurrected.

Healing Power

dst of our dealing with the past there comes a
rful opportunity for us to experience the *healing*
er of the Holy Spirit. Painful memories—which have
never been excavated from our soul—live on the inside
and take up residence deep in our psyche, feeding on
many little things. These experiences can serve as God-
ordained irritants, which will force us to deal with them
once and for all. If properly acknowledged and dealt
with, these irritants can be turned into valuable pearls
that can enhance our future. Without these irritations,
the Holy Spirit would not have the opportunity to deal
with the issues that come to the surface.

These irritations are like the grains of sand which find
their way into the belly of an oyster. Under the micro-
scope, a grain of sand contains sharp jagged edges which
rub against the soft belly of the oyster. Once the oyster
senses this irritation, it secretes a substance known as
"mother of pearl." This liquid substance hardens around
the grand of sand, coating it over and over until the

oyster does not feel the pain from the irritating grain of sand. The result is one of the great marvels of nature—a pearl.

Once we acknowledge the irritation in our lives, the Holy Spirit will aid us by releasing His anointing into that area. The result is that the situation—like the grain of sand—is not moved out of our lives, but we are empowered from deep within to turn our pain into pearls of great value. This process will help us conquer our past and claim our future, and we will experience God's healing and restoring power from the inside out.

A pastor friend of mine shared with me about an experience he had while working as a motorcycle policeman. He was involved in an accident and slid for several feet, scraping the skin from his leg. While he was in the hospital recovering, every few days the nurse would come and take him to sit in a warm whirlpool bath. The warm water softened the scab that had formed and then the nurse pulled it off. This was, as you can imagine, quite a painful process.

After so many of these experiences, my friend cried out, "Why do we have to go through this? It hurts!" The nurse replied, "Reverend, healing occurs from the inside out. By pulling off the softened scab, the healing powers of the body are able to push their way into the area of the wound."

Ah! What a revelation! Yes, healing can be a difficult

process for it will bring to the surface many painful issues, but it affords us the opportunity to allow the Holy Spirit to pull off our old scabs and administer His healing power to our wounds.

Reconciliation

Another area that needs to be touched if we are to be empowered to leave our past behind is *reconciliation*. We need to be at peace with our past and the people who have hurt us before we can move forward so that there will be nothing that keeps us from successfully advancing. We must be resolved that what has happened in the past is just that: "in the past." If not, we will not be able to move with a wholeness in our spirit that allows us to accomplish the present task at hand.

Until we sit under the healing power of the Holy Spirit, we are subject to be bound by flashbacks that keep reminding us of the suffering that we have experienced in the past. These flashbacks can make us cautious and unsure about our future. Although we cannot stop the memories from returning periodically, we can get to a place of peace, which gives us the certainty that we have power over our past. That is a part of reconciliation. Reconciliation is acknowledging the past, knowing that we can't change it, yet having the power to draw from the reservoir of its experiences. In short, reconciliation is a state of knowing how to make your past "pay you."

In the classic movie, *Lion King,* Simba experiences the power of reconciliation with his past. After running away because of being accused of something he really did not do (killing his father Mufasa), he finds himself burying his past in the company of two characters, Timon and Pumba. In their company he tries to obliterate the pain of his past with the activities of his new life. A prophetic figure—Rafiki (a baboon)—who had served Simba's father Mufasa, comes to find Simba. In the scene where they are reunited, Rafiki gets Simba's attention by singing a crazy song. The song irritates Simba but opens the way for them to have a conversation.

"What does that song mean?"
"It means that you are a baboon, and I am not."
"You are confused."
"You are confused. You don't even know who you are.
"And I suppose you do?"
"Sure. You are Mufasa's boy."
"You *knew* my father?"
"Correction, I *know* your father."
"My father died a long time ago."
"Uh uh! He's alive, and I'll show him to you. Follow old Rafiki."

Rafiki leads Simba through a swamp in the darkness of night to a pond. The swamp represents the darkness that comes before the light. It is akin to the night in our lives when we have to face dark issues. Once at the pond the dialogue continues as Rafiki instructs Simba to look into the water. Upon seeing his reflection, he says, "That is not my father." Rafiki challenges him to look harder. This time he sees his father in the reflection as Rafiki shows him that his father lives inside of him. In that scene comes a soliloquy between father and son. In the vision, Mufasa expresses disappointment that Simba has forgotten him, although Simba denies it. Mufasa makes it plain to him that Simba has forgotten his father because he has forgotten who he is. As he departs in the vision, he continues to repeat: "Remember who you are."

After the vision, the lesson of reconciliation with his past is almost complete. Simba now knows that he will have to face his past in order to move on into his future. To help him along, Rafiki hits him on the head with his rod.

Simba asks, "What did you do that for?"
Rafiki responds, "Who cares, it's in the past?"
"Ouch, the past hurts."
"Yes, the past can hurt; but as I see it there are two things you can do: Run from it or learn from it. So, what are you going to do?"

As Simba goes running off into his future, he experiences the reconciling power that comes when you confront your past for what it is. Reconciliation does not change your past. There is nothing that can do that. But, it does help you to be at peace with the woulda, shoulda and coulda syndrome that plagues our present and keeps us from moving into our future.

Another preacher friend of mine told me of a wonderful

story that demonstrates the real life power of reconciliation. One day his daughter, who was in the custody of his ex-wife, called him and said "Daddy, I can't forgive you until you tell my momma you're sorry." He immediately responded by calling his ex-wife and arranging a meeting with her and their three children. There in the presence of his ex-wife and three children he apologized for mistreating his ex-wife while they were together. They prayed and the two were reconciled.

What happened in this case? The daughter was maturing and coming to a place of healing, which allowed her to see that she was carrying a hurt for the way her father had treated her mother. Out of her pain and desire to be healed, she challenged her father to seek reconciliation. Because of his maturity, he was able to positively respond. While we would like to assume that they all got back together and lived happily ever after, that was not what happened. You see, both he and his ex-wife had already remarried and moved on with their lives. "I thought," you may be saying, that "reconciliation put everything back together like it was." No, not necessarily. Sometimes reconciliation can help put things back together, but in this case, as in many situations in life, the ministry of reconciliation may not bring that result because of other decisions we may have made along the way. What is the purpose then, you ask? It's to help us be at peace with what has happened in our past so that we can freely and confidently move on into our future.

Resurrection

There is one more experience that we must have in order to effectively leave our past behind—we will have to be *resurrected*. "But, wait a minute," you might say, "if there is a resurrection, that means someone has to die." That's right. The question is, are you ready to die or are you not sure?

Oftentimes in life there is what I call a "death experience" that precedes the birthing of a new future. Before our vision and dream can come to pass, we must die. "What? You mean I have to die before I live?" Sounds like a Kingdom principle to me. Except the grain of wheat fall to the ground and die, it abides alone (John 12:24). It is out of these "deaths" that an opportunity for new life is created. Through the power of God, we can be resurrected to fulfill our God-given destiny, purpose, and plan even though we have been through devastating times. In this resurrection experience, only God can lead us out of our tombs.

For example, when we experience the death of a loved one, a financial disaster, or some other "death experience," we sometimes are so devastated that we feel we might as well be physically dead. These times are really opportunities for God to resurrect us. They can also serve as a wake-up call for our lives. As the saying goes, "What doesn't kill you, will make you stronger." Many times this is the experience that we need to shock us and make our dream or vision come to life, just as the doctors sometimes use electric shock to make a heart start beating again. It doesn't matter that we have made a series of bad choices which have left us financially devastated and running far behind the pack. It doesn't matter if we have been in and out of so many bad relationships that we wonder if we will ever succeed in one. We must let the past stay in the past because there is more in store for all of us in the future. There *is* life after bankruptcy. There *is* life after divorce. We are candidates for God's resurrection power in our lives.

Out of the ground comes the greatness that God placed in our lives. Out of the tomb—like Lazarus—God calls us forth for a new beginning. Out of the grave—after the designated time—God raises us up in a manifestation where only God gets the glory. "That sounds great," you may be saying, "but I don't like that dying part."

We must realize that until we die (have death type experiences), we are still full of ourselves and our ways. It is only because we have not laid down our old ways that we got into the situation which required God's healing and reconciling power in the first place.

Before Jesus died on the cross, He did what He saw the Father do by working miracles, healing the sick and even raising the dead. The last thing that Jesus did—offering Himself in death—brought Him the greatest eternal honor from His Father. Through the agony of His death, we see the model of how to die to our flesh by pouring ourselves out for the sake of God's will and purpose being accomplished in our lives.

Resurrection opens the door for a new and revised you. After Jesus was resurrected, He came back with ALL power in His hands as it says in Matthew 28:18, "And Jesus came and spake unto them, saying, All power is given unto me in heaven and in earth." This was the reward for the sacrifice of Himself. When we offer ourselves to Him—our will and our plans—God will reward us by bringing our dreams and vision back with new force and power. Without God's resurrection power at work in our lives, we will not be able to forget those things that are behind and move ahead.

> *Brethren, I count not myself to have apprehended: but this one thing I do, forgetting those things which are behind, and reaching forth unto those things which are before, I press toward the mark for the prize of the high calling of God in Christ Jesus* (Philippians 3:13-14).

Arise and Go!

Arise, go over this Jordan, thou, and all this people, unto the land which I do give to them, even to the children of Israel (Joshua 1:2).

The scene in the first chapter of Joshua opens with the people in mourning for their leader Moses who has been called to his eternal home. For 30 days the children of Israel had been mourning at the base of Mt. Nebo. No doubt many of them, especially Joshua and Caleb, remembered their people's slavery in Egypt and the history of their sojourn in the wilderness. The people had made mistakes and disobeyed God's principles. by breaking God's covenant law time after time in the past. Here they were on the verge of moving into the new future that God had been working them toward for over 400 years, but they were still grieving their losses. No doubt there were some woulda, shoulda, couldas that were expressed. After all, it was probably because of their own attitudes that their beloved leader Moses had acted inappropriately and hence was disqualified from entering the land that held so much promise for them all.

In the midst of their grieving, God challenges them to "arise." Arise! Be healed! Be reconciled to your past! Confront your mistakes and learn from them! Put aside your present attitude because there are new opportunities that lie ahead, and you will have to bring your resurrected self to those new opportunities. Moses is dead, and He will not return. Your past is behind you—Egypt, sin, disobedience, rebellion, and the wilderness that held you captive for 40 years. Arise! Arise in your thoughts! Arise in your understanding! Arise in your perception! Drop your excess baggage. Be healed! Be reconciled! Then arise!

The next instruction He had for them and that is valid for us today is to go! "Where?" you may be asking. Toward the future that God has always had in mind for you.

Chapter 2

Didn't I Tell You What To Do?

This Book of the Law shall not depart from your mouth, but you shall meditate in it day and night, that you may observe to do according to all that is written in it. For then you will make your way prosperous, and then you will have good success. "Have I not commanded you? Be strong and of good courage; do not be afraid, nor be dismayed, for the LORD your God is with you wherever you go (Joshua 1:8-9 NKJ).

On Saturday mornings when I was growing up, my mother would leave a chore list posted in one of three places—on the headboard of my bed, on the door of my room, or on the bathroom mirror—where I was bound to see it. At the bottom of the list would be a final message of encouragement: "Do this by the time I get back!" Likewise does God give us His instructions, putting them right before us in His Word.

Sometimes it is hard to move forward with the Lord's commandments, not because what He has told us to do is so hard, but because of the way we perceive it. Our perceptions limit our effective response to the will of God and hence the joy and blessing that come from just doing what He said to do. As we have seen, sometimes we hold onto the past losses, hurts, and disappointments, keeping us on a pathway filled with less and less, although we say that we want more and more. It seems so hard to perform the task, yet He told us, "My yoke is easy and my burden is light" (Matthew 11:30).

Unlike Abraham's faithful actions when challenged to do the will in sacrificing His only Son, many times we remain frozen in the valley of indecision, waiting for some more concrete sign that God will be with us as we move in the thing that God has told us to do. When He speaks, we must immediately assume the attitude of a performer: No matter what the script says, the show must go on. Any other response sets us up for failure.

When we don't move, the appearance of unbelief—and that is what it is—sets off some reactions from the enemy of our souls who now has seen that we are hesitant to follow on with the Lord. When God speaks and tells us to "Leave the past behind," we must be very careful not to even bring up for discussion the hurts, pains, and losses of the past. While there may still be places where reconciliation and restoration work needs to take place, we can't make our past into our present occupation. As long as the enemy knows that we are living in the past, he will taunt us and tempt us not to obey the Lord. As long as the enemy knows that we are dwelling on what has already happened, he can distract us from seeing the present move of God in our lives. When God says "Drop it!" we need to exhibit the right attitude by" forgetting those things that are behind…and press toward the mark of the prize of the high calling which is in Christ Jesus."

Some people say, "I'll forgive, but I won't forget." Fortunately, that is not God's attitude about our past. When God forgives us, He releases us from the burden of our past and frees us to accomplish our destiny. When God forgives us, we need to agree with Him. When God releases us from our past, we need to agree with Him. When God speaks, our conversation should change. If we don't talk about the past, we will give no one else any fuel for distracting and unproductive conversation. Since the tongue is an unruly member which can run our ship into the rocks of life, we should be prayerful to "set a watch" on our mouth. That is why God encourages Joshua to "meditate on the law" both day and night. When our thoughts change, then so too will our conversation which precedes our actions.

Filter Our Thoughts

The Apostle Paul, whom I call the apostle of the mind, challenges us to filter the thoughts that fill our minds.

Finally, brethren, whatsoever things are true, whatsoever things are honest, whatsoever things are just, whatsoever things are pure, whatsoever things are lovely, whatsoever things are of good report; if there be any virtue, and if

14

there be any praise, think on these things
(Philippians 4:8-9 KJV).

I like to translate it this way: "If it does not meet the
test, then in your mind don't let it rest." In other words,
it will not lead to the fulfillment of the will of God and
your purpose in life.

The Rotary Club has a wonderful set of criteria that un-
derscores this principle. They call it the Four Way Test
of Agreement. It reads as follows:

Is it true? It is fair? Is it beneficial? Will it promote
goodwill and better friendships?

In other words, if what we are thinking and saying does
not align with these principles, then we shouldn't say it!
We need to stop wasting precious time thinking and
talking about things that do not contribute toward the
fulfillment of our real desire: to reach the Promised
Land of our lives. We need to stop letting distractions
steal from the precious resource of our time.

I was in my office one day before the "do not call list"
was created. A salesman called and wanted to schedule
an appointment to see me. I graciously responded that I
would be willing to review any information that he
would send at my leisure. The salesman was persistent
in his quest for a face-to-face meeting. As forcefully as I
could be without seeming rude, I said to him, "I can't let
you steal my time. I have something I must do." We
can't afford to lose any more time. We have something

that we must do. We are standing on the bank of our blessing—our Jordan river—and cannot let the devil or anyone else steal from us what we have worked so hard to get so that we can make it across the river. It would be a shame for us to have to turn around now, especially since the devil has already tricked us in the past and wasted so much of our valuable time already.

Be Strong and Courageous

Be strong and of a good courage: for unto this people shalt thou divide for an inheritance the land, which I sware unto their fathers to give them. Only be thou strong and very courageous, that thou mayest observe to do according to all the law, which Moses my servant commanded thee: turn not from it to the right hand or to the left, that thou mayest prosper whithersoever thou goest. Have not I commanded thee? Be strong and of a good courage; be not afraid, neither be thou dismayed: for the LORD thy God is with thee whithersoever thou goest (Joshua 1:6-7,9).

In the above verses, the commandment to be "strong" and "courageous" are repeated to Joshua. Maybe the Lord did not see Joshua moving quickly enough to follow Him into his prepared destiny. I don't know for sure, but I can compare the tenor of the text to when my mother returned on Saturday mornings and my "chore list" was not completed. You see, while I had my instructions, I also had the opportunity to use my time in the manner I saw fit. I could either watch Bugs Bunny and Road

Runner and then complete my chores or do my work and then watch Space Ghost and Johnny Quest. The choice was mine. On a few occasions when I chose to delay my work, I would not get all of the chores completed in time for mother's return. When inspection time came—and it will always come—I could hear her ask me, "Didn't I tell you what to do?"

I think that God saw the same kind of hesitation in Joshua, hence the repetition of the command. When God does not see Joshua looking like he is going to follow His commands, He asks him a question in verse 9: "Have not I commanded thee?" When God speaks, there is a certain disposition we should have to immediately move toward the blessing that awaits. The demonstration of any other attitude leaves us open for rebuke from the Lord, delays our destiny, and brings attack from the enemy of our soul.

The command, "Be strong," when translated directly from the Hebrew, means "to fasten upon, to seize, to be obstinate." To be obstinate? Yes. When we have the revelation about our future, we must be obstinate about it. We must resolve that the enemy won't distract us and even our friends will not delay us. We cannot give away any time! We must pursue the conquest of our possession. What about courage? It translates into being "alert," both physically and mentally. We must be ready for the journey into our destiny. It is an exciting adventure that will afford us the opportunity to conquer many heights. Our body and mind must be in sync with our

17

spirit. Wholeness is the key. Not that there won't be challenges that stir up our inner fears, but we will recognize those fears and know that God will see us through.

Joshua also is commanded, "Do not be afraid." In other words, we can't let our fears (false evidence appearing real) harass us. That's right. "Don't be afraid" translates into not being harassed by our fears. David cried out in Psalm 34:4, "I sought the LORD, and he heard me, and delivered me from all my fears." Like David, we are going to be in some situations that will make us afraid. It is alright to acknowledge to the Lord that we are afraid. After that confession, however, we need to be ready to receive God's divine strength which will fortify us for the conquest. When we face our future, we shouldn't sweat it! We are a conqueror and much more than a conqueror.

Another command for Joshua is: "Neither be dismayed!" The root of the word "dismayed" means to prostrate oneself or to be so terrified that we fall down. To turn back is easy. We know what is there. But to move forward toward our possession? Now there's something that could make us pass out. You might say, "My past has been so dismal that I cannot possibly be expected to believe that God sees my destiny is still possible." Yes, He does. "But it is too great!" Yes it is. God called us for greatness, but the plan was temporarily interrupted. However God is still prodding us along toward the greatness He prepared. He is gently asking us the following question because He has an expectation for our lives: "Didn't I tell you what to do?" We must, therefore, arise and do it!

Chapter 3

He's Already Made a Way

And as soon as we heard these things, our hearts melted; neither did there remain any more courage in anyone because of you, for the LORD your God, He is God in heaven above and on earth beneath (Joshua 2:11 NKJ).

Sometimes we are in a position to be blessed and yet do not recognize the good things that God is about to do for us. We cannot see God's hand because we see ourselves in a different light than He does. Our own perspective of ourselves can hinder our conquest of territory that God has prepared for us to possess. To conquer new territory and possess our destiny, we must come to understand that God has something on His mind that He wants to accomplish through us. BIG GOD and little us! That is the key. What about the little us?

Many Christians have adopted the attitude that feeling good about themselves is proud and arrogant. If we intend to conquer and possess our destiny, however, we will have to have a positive self-picture. That self-picture is a reflection of Christ that shines through us to accomplish God's purpose in our lives. While it is true that we should "let another praise (us) and not your own mouth," we should also know that like our Brother, Christ Jesus, "it is not robbery to make yourself equal with God." After all, we are His children and heirs to all that He has.

Now we must be careful not to get worked up thinking that we are something that we are not and thereby deceive ourselves. The fact remains, however, that with the anointing in our lives, we are not just *ordinary* anymore—we are *special*.

A Royal Priesthood

But ye are a chosen generation, a royal priesthood, an holy nation, a peculiar people; that ye should shew forth the praises of him who hath called you out of darkness into his marvellous light (1 Peter 2:9).

We are part of a royal priesthood. Truly, the anointing makes the difference in our lives. It is the difference between what we are not and what God destined for us to be.

When we receive salvation and the power of the Holy Spirit in our lives, we are positioned for a greatness we have never experienced. Just imagine, the God of the universe dwells in our mortal bodies. As Paul said,

But we have this treasure in earthen vessels, that the excellency of the power may be of God, and not of us (2 Corinthians 4:7).

What a claim to fame: great big God lives in little ole us. Right now, we are who God says we are. When God points us out in a crowd, we shouldn't look around for someone else to fulfill the great destiny that He is setting before us. God is talking to us. Yes, us! He wants to use us, He wants to anoint us, and He wants to bless us.

When I was saved and called to the ministry, I was full of zeal and excitement about what God wanted to do in my life. My dreams were big and bold. Somewhere in between then and now, my dreams were tested and tried. Many of them died along with many of my desires. For a period of time, I even lost sight of the fact that I had something BIG I wanted to do for the Lord. That is just where God wanted me—on the cross emptied of myself. I had to die to me so that I could see HIM! I had to die to my view of me so that I could see His view of me. I had to die to my purpose so that I could see that His purpose was bigger. Then when "i" (small case intended) saw HIM, God released the anointing to secure His destiny for me.

Now some years later, the fire burns hotter than ever, only this time it burns with more intentional direction. I understand better His anointing upon my life. It is really not about me. When the "you" gets out of the way, then you will be able to see HIM. That is when God reveals His purpose for your life. What a joy it is to discover the power of one's purpose in life. In the words of the old hymn, it was "at the cross where I first saw the light."

It is also at the cross where we will continue to have the light of His revelation for our lives uncovered. It is in this place that God will reveal what has been there all the while. It is in this place that we will come to find out that God has already made a way for greatness in our lives. He was just waiting on us to come to maturity. He was waiting for us to see HIM and not ourselves.

The Power of Our Destiny

For the first time in their journey, the Israelites come face to face with the power of their destiny when they were about ready to cross the Jordan. They are the rightful possessors of the land of Canaan. Unlike their forefathers some 40 years earlier, they now see the magnitude of greatness that God has put within them by His divine providence. Unlike their forefathers who concluded that they did not have the ability to conquer the land because of the giants, this new generation sees itself in a healthier perspective. We too can do what He said we can do. Why? Not because of who we are, but because of who GOD is. They realized that their conquest was not about them, but about HIM and so must we.

Forty years earlier, Moses had sent out twelve spies. This time Joshua sent out only two. Remember it was just two of the twelve (Joshua and Caleb) who came back with a good report about their ability to conquer the land. This time Joshua made sure that there could be no negative majority opinion to make the heart of the Israelites faint. Over the last 40 years, this new generation came to appreciate the God of provision in a new way. This new generation had not been mentally abused and beaten down by slavery. They had been born free, and although they wandered in the wilderness for 40 years, they lived a different kind of lifestyle. They saw water come out of a rock, quails fall out of the sky, and manna on the grass in the morning. All of these experiences reinforced the fact that they were special. After all, there were no other people to their knowledge that ever had this kind of treatment.

These miraculous experiences caused them to place a different value not only on God and their leader but also on themselves. They saw themselves as special and believed that they were in fact destined to inherit the land that the Lord had promised was theirs. They had a different mindset about the God of their heritage and themselves. They recognized the power of God's anointing upon their lives and its effect. They recognized also how others viewed them. God's anointing upon their lives made their enemies afraid of what they might do next. God's anointing upon their lives put fear in the hearts of their enemies. The children were confident, not in themselves, but in the power of God to bring to pass His plan for their lives.

When you know who you are and what you're anointed to do, you are dangerous! You are unstoppable! You are ready to become a conqueror and more than a conqueror—you are ready to possess your inheritance. The only thing that is standing in the way of the fulfillment of your destiny is you. The territory that is yours has already surrendered to you because of God's anointing upon your life. God has already made a way. All you have to do is see Him at work and work with Him.

Chapter 4

Make Me (Rahab) An Offer You (Israelites) Can't Refuse

So the men said to her: "We will be blameless of this oath of yours which you have made us swear, "unless, when we come into the land, you bind this line of scarlet cord in the window through which you let us down, and unless you bring your father, your mother, your brothers, and all your father's household to your own home. "So it shall be that whoever goes outside the doors of your house into the street, his blood shall be on his own head, and we will be guilt-less. And whoever is with you in the house, his blood shall be on our head if a hand is laid on him. "And if you tell this business of ours, then we will be free from your oath which you made us swear." Then she said, "According to your words, so be it." And she sent them away, and they departed. And she bound the scarlet cord in the window (Joshua 2:17-21 NKJ).

While we are on the cross dying to self, someone else has been watching God's prepa-ration for our destiny. It is not unusual for others to recognize before we do that God is preparing to do great things in our lives. Perhaps when we were young, folks would declare that they could see something special about us. That is an outward sign of God's stamp upon our lives. The time from revelation to realization is our wilderness—our season of testing, trial, suffering, and preparation.

God's Creative Plan

The text in the latter part of Joshua 2 unveils an unlikely character in the plan of God. I believe that this encounter with Rahab the harlot is part of God's lesson for us. God's plan is always bigger than our situations and circumstances. The two spies that Joshua sent came upon the city of Jericho with its fortified walls. One of the prostitutes in the city recognized these strangers as being from the Hebrew company that she had heard was wandering in the wilderness for 40 years.

She recognized the anointing upon their lives because she had heard about it for quite some time. She heard about how they were sustained in the wilderness for 40 years—that even their shoes and their clothes did not wear out! She heard that they did not have to buy groceries but ate manna and quail, which were divinely provided. And she heard that they did not have to worry about their water supply in the desert for their God had made water come out of a rock! So, what did she do? She decided to join in with God's anointed people. She enlisted them to make an offer that she could not refuse. In doing so she secured her future and the future of her family. What were the benefits? Immediately she and her family were saved. Futuristically she became the great—great—great—great—great (and so on) grand-mother of Jesus, but that is another story. There are some things that we can learn from this story that will affect our future as we move forward into the fulfillment of our destiny.

1) Be sincere in our desire.

Rahab was sincere about her need—she wanted deliverance for herself and her family. We can't waste people's time trying to get help on our terms. In Matthew 13 we find the story of a Greek woman who came to Jesus seeking help for her daughter who was sick. Jesus responded to the woman that He could not in good conscience give the children's bread (healing) to dogs. Awful! The Palestinian Teacher called this Greek woman a dog. The literal translation reads "hound" dog. Humph! She was not even a purebred. Mind you now, it was not that Jesus was prejudiced against non-Jews, He was merely voicing the sentiments of the crowd around Him so that He could show them the pitiful estate of their religious tradition.

Well, how did the woman respond in order to conquer this prejudice? With faith! She acknowledged who and where she was and still insisted that she had a right to receive what she was asking for. Amazing! Jesus counted the sincerity of her desire as faith. The result: she received her desire. When we want something bad enough, we will do whatever it takes to get it.

2) Listen to the instructions for deliverance.

Just because we can identify our problem, it doesn't mean that we can solve it ourselves. That is what generally got us into the situation in the first place—trying to solve our problems on our own. We must hear God's voice. It is what we hear that determines what we think, which in turn dictates what we speak and how we act.

We need to be careful of the voices that we listen to. Many would-be, self-appointed advisers may mean well, but they may not have the word that we need to help us get out of the situation that we are in. There are many who will say to us, "If I were you, here is what I would do." But that is the problem—they are not you, and have never been in your situation. What God has destined for your life is just for you.

God, however, sometimes does reveal His plan through someone else, as in the case of Rahab. But when our divine instruction comes, we need to be very careful to pay attention to it. It is for our life. Hearing implies "doing" and "obedience." The instructions may be as simple as "keep quiet" or as complex as a plan for saving us from our enemies, but they are for our deliverance.

3) Help someone else with their dilemma.

One of the responsibilities of receiving is that we must give to others what we have been blessed to receive. We must do good when it is in the power of our hands to do it. If God helps us out of a situation, then we must try to assist someone else in their dilemma. God does not de-

27

liver us just for us, but so that we can be examples or witnesses for others to see the goodness of God. If we won't let our light shine, then why should God give us a bigger candle?

In Luke 10 we see the parable of the Good Samaritan who had compassion for someone else's misfortune. The Samaritan himself was disenfranchised from society. He was considered by the Judean Jews as a half-breed. But the Lord had blessed Him, and he recognized that the blessing in his own life needed to be shared with others regardless of their ethnic origin. This Samaritan used his resources to glorify God by helping someone in their time of need. God had been so good to him that he wanted to be good to someone else. When God brings us into our inheritance, we shouldn't forget to help someone else with their situation.

4) Follow all His directions.
The way to our deliverance may not make sense at first to *us*. It may take *us* into unknown areas. Generally God uses this to "stretch *our* faith" to new heights. Sometimes not only will the instructions take *us* to new heights, they will also take *us* to new places or cities as in my example below.

I had just returned from a one-week revival that had turned into a three-week crusade in Kingston, Jamaica. The Lord had blessed mightily. I left Jamaica heading straight for Chicago for some meetings. After preaching for a pastor friend of mine in Evanston, I rested for a few days in the comforts of his home. On that Tuesday morning, he and his wife took me to the airport to catch a flight home to Florida. While standing in line to check in for the flight, the Lord spoke to me and told me to "go to Milwaukee." In my mind, I tried to justify why I should not go. Lack of funds was one of the reasons that floated into my head.

I stood there with my bags and watched the other passengers board the plane. The doors closed, the jet pulled away and taxied from the gate. Soon I was settled in a rental car driving to Milwaukee. (Had I been more in tune with God's directions, I would have just caught the train. I eventually had to return the car to Chicago and then catch the train back to Milwaukee.) A few hours later I checked into a hotel. I had no contacts in the city—I had never been there before—so I called another pastor friend in Indiana. He told me of a preacher and gave me a phone number. When I spoke with the preacher—an assistant pastor at his church—he informed me that he was expecting a guest revivalist on the coming week but that he would see what other doors for ministry might be available.

Four days later, he took me out to dinner along with some other ministers. As he was dropping me back at the hotel on that Friday night, he assured me that a door for ministry would open for me and that his guest evangelist would be in on the following day. The Lord spoke to me as I was stepping out of the van: "He's (the guest evangelist) not coming." The next morning the Lord awakened me with another instruction: "Check out of the hotel, call the preacher, and tell him you need a place to stay." As I mulled around in my head all the reasons why I should not follow this instruction, the realization that my funds were about exhausted motivated me to make the call. A few hours later, after some of the deacons had picked me up, I was in the living room of the preacher's home. As they were preparing lunch, I could hear the preacher in the back room on the phone saying "That's alright...that's alright, I have a preacher sitting right here in my living room, and now I know why the Lord sent him." The call was from the office of the scheduled evangelist informing the preacher that he would not be able to come.

As you may have already guessed, the guest evangelist for the entire week-long revival was yours truly. What happened in that meeting was nothing short of miraculous. In the first service, God healed a woman of a herniated disc in her spine. In the second service (Sunday night), God saved the nephew of the preacher. His testimony will forever encourage me to follow God's instructions exactly. "Preacher," he said, "on the morning you were standing in the Chicago airport, I was getting out of jail. I know that God had to send you to this city just for me." To God be the glory!

When we follow God's directions, we will obtain what we need. Not only will we be blessed, but someone else's blessing may also be awaiting our obedience.

5) Express faith in His decision.
Rahab declared her faith in the instructions by saying

Amen! So be it. If we say what God says, we will get the results He gets. It is just that simple. We must speak affirmatively about God's plan and instructions for our lives. It may seem impossible to our friends. It may appear impractical to our family, but we must affirm God's decisions for our lives and speak well of our destiny.

Then our faith must move us to follow the instructions. What did Rahab do? She tied the red cord in her window. What did this accomplish? It identified her as one who is radical enough, one who is simplistic enough, one who is faithful enough to follow the Lord all the way. God said it. I believe it. That settles it. What did this woman do? She got God (through His servants) to make her an offer of deliverance that she could not refuse.

Finally, you may ask the question, what did God see in the red cord? He definitely saw something He liked. He saw the color of the blood! Do you remember the deliverance of the children of Israel from Egyptian slavery when they put the blood of lambs on the doorposts? What happened when the angel of death came through the camp? The angel passed over every house where there was the blood of the lamb.

What about the Blood of the Lamb? When we come to the Father under the covering of the blood of His Son our Savior, He is constrained to release us and honor our offer. It is an offer that He can't refuse. As the old saints would say, "Just put it under the blood."

Chapter 5

On the Verge of a Breakthrough

Early in the morning Joshua and all the Israelites set out from Shittim and went to the Jordan, where they camped before crossing over (Joshua 3:1 NIV).

Sometimes we can be on the verge of being blessed, but because we do not realize God's desire toward us, we can become side-tracked from the wonderful thing that God wants to do. Have you ever noticed that it is when *you* are about to go into another place—a new dimension or blessing—that everything comes to distract *you* from what God is doing?

It is the pleasure of God to give us the kingdom. It is His pleasure to give us mountain-moving power so that He may be glorified. Many times we have stopped short of the place where God is taking us because of fear, habit, or ignorance.

FEAR—False Evidence Appearing Real

We are afraid of the unknown. God is taking us somewhere we have never been before and stretching us to new limits. We are afraid to go on an adventure with the Spirit. We need to not only say He is our guide, but also trust Him to lead us to "boldly go where no man has gone before." Change is challenging but not impossible.

Some of us would rather break than yield to the new thing that God wants to do in us. God won't break us, but we break and tear when we don't yield. It sometimes bothers us when God is trying to change our habits because we are comfortable with them. But we need to come to the place where we concede that the way we have been doing things has not kept pace with the demands of His plans for us.

God, who exists in the past, present, and future, is on the cutting edge of change and precisely assesses and knows man's needs. Should not the saints who say that they know Him, also be on the cutting edge of change and development for the good of humanity? We should be leading and showing the world how to change by our example of being willing to move with the current mind of the Spirit. After all, is change not what we are supposed to be preaching? That is what salvation is all about! Why do we complain about going through changes? How is it that after we are changed—saved—we can so easily get stuck and decide not to move any further. The world is not knocking at our door to be saved. Oftentimes unbelievers see more progress—motion—movement—in the world than they do in the church. The heathen don't want to get stuck in the old habit and ineffective rituals that they see Christians sometimes mired in.

I believe that one of my trademark sayings will help you understand what I am saying (the first two lines are not originally mine).

If you always do what you have always done,
you will always have what you always had.
If you always go where you have always gone,
you will always be where you have always been.

If you always see what you have always seen,
you will always know what you have always known.
If you always give what you have always given,
you will always reap what you have always reaped.

See nothing! Know nothing!
Go nowhere! Be nowhere!
Do nothing! Have nothing!
Sow nothing! Reap nothing!

In the story I previously shared about going to Milwaukee, the experience made me confront my fears of the unknown. It also made me change my habits and move freely with the liberating force of the Holy Spirit behind me. I had an opportunity to do something new. I had an opportunity to go somewhere I had never been before. I had an opportunity to see God do a new thing. I had an opportunity to sow and reap something I had never reaped before. It was glorious.

Moreover, through this experience, I was enlightened in God's Word. This chapter's message came while I was sitting in the assistant pastor's home. Had I not been obedient, I would never have come into this knowledge. This was an opportunity for me to be enlightened. This was an opportunity for me to be freed from the bondage of my own ignorance. This was an opportunity for me to experience a breakthrough in my life and ministry that would carry me to new heights and dimensions.

I could have easily continued on my journey home following my own plan. Just as the children of Israel, I was camped on the border of my blessing—the verge of my breakthrough. You, too are on the verge of a breakthrough. God is ready to take you across your Jordan to a new place of blessing. You have a decision to make. Are you going to turn around and go back to what you know? That is safe—maybe. Or are you going to cross over into the unknown and conquer your fears and habits and allow the Holy Spirit to dispel your ignorance?

It is time for you to step across your Jordan into the Promised Land. God does not want you to turn back like the generation who had been slaves in Egypt. They wandered in the wilderness for 40 years and died never inheriting the blessing that God had promised them.

God loves you and that is why He has been stretching you. Now the Lord is ready to walk you into your possession. He is empowering you to take what is yours. You are on the verge of a breakthrough!

Chapter 6

We're Crossing Over!

Then the priests who bore the ark of the covenant of the LORD stood firm on dry ground in the midst of the Jordan; and all Israel crossed over on dry ground, until all the people had crossed completely over the Jordan (Joshua 3:17 NKJ).

Well, it is time! You have been on the edge of your Jordan long enough. Crossing over is necessary, although I know that it is more comfortable where you are.

Everyone is comfortable in familiar surroundings, but the truth is that all of us need to move on. Staying in the wilderness too long will negatively impact our thinking. If we don't get out now, we will be stuck for the rest of our lives. It's not too late to make a new decision for a better future, but we better hurry up.

The wilderness was good for us. It helped to develop our character and teach us many valuable lessons. But the wilderness is only the temporary provision that comes before the promised possession. The wilderness shows us that God can do miraculous things; there we are out of slavery but have not yet reached our destination. In the wilderness God tests us to get us ready to inherit the greater blessing that He has for us. The journey is what makes us ready for the next level of blessing.

In the wilderness, the only enemy that the children of Israel were fighting was themselves. They had good leadership and were on their way to a better place. But in the wilderness, the slave mentality that was in them needed to be purged out. Forty years earlier, the newly freed slaves had missed their opportunity to immediately enter the Promised Land, not because of available resources or abilities and not because they lacked the presence of an omnipotent God. They missed coming into their possession because their own minds limited them from moving any further in life. The greatest enemy is not *around* us but *within* us. We are our own hindrance. As we think in our heart, so it is to us.

It Is Required

Well, not only does there come a time to enter into our inheritance, but it is required. Why? God has willed our success, and His plan does not call for an extended stay outside of His plan. God wants us out! Out of what? He wants us out of the wilderness. He longs to shower His blessings upon us. His will is for us to become His vessel of praise in the earth. He wants us to be His reflection to a dying hurting world. To bring that about, He must position us for greatness. It is from this position that He will

37

use us to be His light in the world. He brings us out, to get us through, to bring us to, to set us up, to bring others out. That is the circle of blessing. He wants to do so much for us that He will take us out kicking and screaming if He has to, just to get us to the blessing. His words of assurance ring out in Luke 12 when He assured the disciples who are seeking the kingdom of God that it is indeed "your Father's good pleasure to give you the kingdom."

Well, who is required to come out? Everybody! God moves individually, but He also moves corporately. There are some blessings that will come just because we are "in the number." We are individually responsible for our own spirituality and are all at different spiritual levels. God knows that. However, there are some corporate blessings that are not based upon that. They are based upon God's sovereign decision and timing for "His people."

To make sure that we share in the responsibility for everyone around us, in particular the household of faith, God asks a question: "Where is your brother? Where is your sister?" We cannot be like Cain and respond that we do not know. We have a responsibility to challenge the spiritual level of each member of the household of faith. When we know that God is blessing the house, we shouldn't let our brothers and sisters miss out on what God has ordered for all of us.

Take the risk and hold your fellow Christians accountable for their life. If you really love them as you say you do, then tell them what you believe will help them. If you see areas in their lives that need improving, then reach out to them and help them. When your brother or sister comes to you in love to help you correct areas of your life, don't respond to them by noting the areas of their life that you see, receive what they say in the spirit of love and pray about it. Later, you may return the favor and bring to their attention something they need to work on.

In the text, the leaders were told to go through the camp and tell everyone to sanctify themselves. They were instructed to encourage the people to get ready for the move of God. Encourage your neighbors to sanctify themselves, both through your words and by what you do yourself. Share with them how to get ready for the move of God by doing a spiritual checkup.

It was through the leadership of Joshua that the corporate blessings flowed down to the people. As the head aligns itself with God's divine purpose, so the house must come into alignment as well. The priests were the first to step into the waters of the Jordan—into uncharted territory. They were the first from this younger generation to experience God's divine power in this manner since the older generation that had crossed the Red Sea had died out. As the priests—leaders—stood in the place of God's blessing, so the people realized God's blessings for their lives. In this lies a wonderful admonishment for leadership as well as for the members of household of faith.

First, God's leaders must be sanctified and obedient to step into places where they have never trod before. If the people of God are going to arrive at the place of their possession, leaders must be willing to sacrifice to help get them there. Secondly, the members of the household of faith must be willing to submit to God-directed leadership so that they can get to the place of their possession. Since you have never "crossed this way before" you must be willing to allow those that God has anointed to help you get where you need to go. The result is a spiritual balance and interdependency that helps us all to achieve the accomplishment of our dreams and the fulfillment of our destiny.

Chapter 7

Daddy, Wazzup Wid Dat?

That this may be a sign among you when your children ask in time to come, saying, "What do these stones mean to you?" Then you shall answer them that the waters of the Jordan were cut off before the ark of the covenant of the LORD; when it crossed over the Jordan, the waters of the Jordan were cut off. And these stones shall be for a memorial to the children of Israel forever (Joshua 4:6-7 NKJ).

L egacy is the opportunity of the future, which was created by the work of the past and remembered and celebrated in the present. It is the heritage of tomorrow that is set up today by those who had foresight yesterday.

Twenty-twenty hindsight is the easiest to have. It is easy to see what you should have done yesterday to have a different today which would make your tomorrow come out with a different ending. Many people are living in regret because of the today they now experience which was created by the mistakes of their yesterdays. Woulda, coulda, shouldas can eat up your today and make you miss your opportunity for a better tomorrow.

Tomorrow is not necessarily promised (unless God specifies it so), so don't waste your today commiserating over your yesterdays. This does nothing but rob you of your tomorrow. When you are working on legacy—the opportunity for the future created by the past and celebrated today—it makes you look at these three dimensions all at the same time. Effective legacy planning involves looking at your past, present, and your future through the guidance of the Holy Spirit.

God gives insight to a person or group of people to begin a project or launch an organization that will grow bigger and endure longer than they can individually. When God gives a vision, it always has a three-dimensional effect. It *re-charts* your past (God's plan always has power over your past), it *energizes* your present, and it *enhances* your future. If your vision is only capable of suiting your today, it is not from God.

The African Methodist Episcopal Church, where I am privileged to serve as an itinerant elder, was started by less than a dozen people who were committed to growing something that would endure longer than they. Bishop Richard Allen, who founded the church in 1787 in a blacksmith shop, was determined to provide a place for African Americans to worship freely. Although I am quite sure that he foresaw a church enduring beyond his present capacity to lead, I don't know whether he envisioned the church of the 21st century with nearly 5,000 churches on four continents with a membership of over 2.5 million, along with 19 colleges & universities as well. Beginning his life as a slave, the fact that he purchased his freedom through the help of the Masons and then became the first African American bishop on the continent of America, as well as the first bishop of the oldest African American organization was probably not on his mind 200 plus years ago. His vision not only suited his today but continues to enhance the "todays" of millions who have come after him.

It definitely is challenging when we look at our past to believe that we can have a different future. It is difficult to believe, in light of our past, that we can establish a legacy that will bless those that come after us. I have experienced many deficit creating circumstances that many times make it difficult for me to believe that any good can come from the mess I have made of my life. But I take courage in the Word that, through the power of the Holy Spirit, I can conquer my past tragedies, reclaim my present, and move into a future with a different outcome. Not that we will escape the boundaries of God's principles of sowing and reaping—no one is above that. But, God's abundant grace is sufficient for us in the worst circumstances to do for us what we cannot do for ourselves. God's grace is a "barrier" between us and the consequences. Not that the consequences will not be there, but His power will not let them overcome us to the point of permanent paralysis.

It is imperative that we live our today in preparation for both ours and someone else's tomorrow. No matter where we are in the development of our legacy, we must begin to build upon the successes and even failures born of our past.

When we measure our present works against the contributions of the past, we often come up short. Our foreparents did so much with so little. Now it seems we do so much less with so much more. Our fathers and mothers built churches and schools with pennies, and we can't seem to keep them open with millions of dollars at our disposal. They went to the banks with pennies in jars and handkerchiefs, and bought and built buildings. Today we have online banking, credit lines, and platinum cards and are not keeping pace proportionately with the accomplishments which our predecessors set. We must be careful not to diminish the importance of the work of the founders by not fueling the progressive continuum.

Our todays are made available for us both to have present enjoyment and to plan our tomorrows. We should not regress into comfort and complacency and just sit where we are, patting ourselves on the back saying that "We have arrived." Just because we are better off than our parents were does not mean that our children will be better off than us. We must work at it. Too many sacrificed for us to be where we are. The spirit of legacy requires that we sacrifice and prepare for the next generation.

Nowhere more so than in the life of the church do we see a generational complacency. In the way we structure our organizations and develop our ministries, we talk the language of growth but walk the language of exclusion. We say we want our church to grow, but we exclude others from participating in the growth process. When some of us hold onto three or four positions in the church, we diminish our effect and exclude others from the work of the present which insures the future. As long as we are taking up all the present opportunities, we will block others from learning and preparing for tomorrow. One of the mistakes my preceding generation made was to label my generation the "church of tomorrow." In response to that my generation said to the established church, "See ya tomorrow." When tomorrow came, many from my generation could not return because they had been taken captive by the bondage of this world. In order for the church to grow, the leaders of today must share responsibility with those of the younger generation. After all, it is God's work. When we try to control it and keep it held tightly in our hands, it won't be able to breathe and take on new life. Leaders must work on our replacements now, to ensure progress tomorrow. Anything less than that will cause stagnation and condemn the church to death.

Likewise, in your life, you will have to release yourself into God's care to bring about the future legacy that you desire. I know that it is hard. It will mean crossing over into your tomorrow and allowing the Holy Spirit to redefine who you think you are. In that redefining comes the liberty to become who God intended for you to be all the while. You can do it! Start today. As a matter of fact all any of us have is today. Get ready for your tomorrow, today! But as it is written:

> *"Eye has not seen, nor ear heard, Nor have entered into the heart of man The things which God has prepared for those who love Him." But God has revealed them to us through His Spirit. For the Spirit searches all things, yes, the deep things of God* (1 Corinthians 2:9-10 NKJ).

If we are indeed walking in the Spirit and allowing ourselves to be led by the Spirit, then the future is certain. We will have an enduring legacy that fulfills us and guarantees the future for our children or successors.

Our plans for today pale in comparison to God's plans for our tomorrows. God has some stuff so big and bold that He can't release the information to us yet because it would overload our possibility circuits. That is why God prepares leaders and gives them three-dimensional vision capacity. They see the past, which is the record of the work of those who preceded them. They see the present situation and help us to celebrate it. They see the future based on the past and present and declare what it can be. Then from their vantage point, they can speak boldly and declare to us that "the best is yet to come."

In the text in Joshua, God is helping Joshua to develop a legacy. By having him bring stones from the river—God teaches Joshua the importance of connecting with the past. The stones are a reminder that will provoke questions by the children as to their meaning, imparting the power of the past to those whose future will extend beyond Joshua's. This inter-generational interaction is important if we are to be successful in our future. Someone else has been where we are trying to go—at least in principle. The bridge to our future is paved with the triumphs and tragedies of our yesterdays. These stones should be set up as reminders for us and for generations to come that only a God could have brought us to this point of success and deliverance.

Look at your past and learn from it. Celebrate your today. It's all you have. Plan and prioritize for your future. When your children ask you "Daddy, wazzup wid dat? Momma, wazzup wid dat? Nanna, wazzup wid dat? Paw paw, wazzup wid dat?" You will be able to tell them, "I'm glad you asked. Let me tell you about the Lord who brought me from a mighty long way."

Chapter 8

Now That We're Over

Then Joshua circumcised their sons whom He raised up in their place; for they were uncircumcised, because they had not been circumcised on the way. So it was, when they had finished circumcising all the people, that they stayed in their places in the camp till they were healed. Then the LORD said to Joshua, "This day I have rolled away the reproach of Egypt from you." Therefore the name of the place is called Gilgal to this day (Joshua 5:7-9 NKJ).

Well, we have crossed over. What does that mean? It means we have a fresh start... a new beginning...a new opportunity to get started on our destiny. God is the God of another chance. I know that the saying reads "second chance," but for many, we blew our second, third, and even fourth chances. So, we'll just let Him be the God of another chance. What is the first order of business when we cross over? Circumcision! There were some things that many of us did not get on the other side. What? You mean I still have something that I need to offer God? Yes.

For the children of Israel, circumcision was the outward sign that they were in covenant with Him. The generation that had crossed over had not been circumcised. They had wandered in the wilderness with their parents who had been circumcised in Egypt. Now, this generation came along who had never known the old ways and the first order of business for them was a revival of the spiritual practices that had brought them across an uncross able river to the border of their blessing.

There are some spiritual practices—fellowship, prayer, fasting—that are always appropriate in the life of the believer. We simply can't make it to the next level without them. To lay them aside is to pronounce death on our Christian walk. When God supernaturally brings us across into another place in Him, we must revive these spiritual practices in order to sustain our deliverance. A daily walk with God will ensure that we do not wander aimlessly as others may have done before us. While we are in the midst of a healing moment, we have the opportunity to ponder our future and reflect upon the past that God has delivered us from.

After this, it is time for a "good, ole fashioned" revival. The Israelites kept the Passover in the plains of Jericho, something they had not done in quite some time. In this 21st century of high-tech worship services and televangelism, seeking the presence of God is still what God has always said it should be. The prophet's words today are just as relevant as they were over 2,400 years ago, "Seek the Lord while He may be found; call upon Him while He is near" (Isaiah 55:6).

It was important for the generation who were finally entering the Promised Land to understand how to get to the heart of God. And it is important for us to know how to get to the heart of God too. For the Israelites, the Passover celebration held the remembrances of how to be in the presence of God. It reminded them of God's love and favor as He stretched forth His hand to deliver His people. Remember how it was when you first came to know the Lord? Do you remember the revival, the prayer meeting, the Bible study where you accepted Him as your personal Savior? As one popular gospel song put it so many years ago, "Take me back, take me Lord to the place where I first received you."

Provision Ceases

Another amazing thing that happened once the children of Israel crossed over is that the manna ceased after they were circumcised, healed, and had held a service of remembrance (Passover). Why? So that the children of Israel could arise and take their possession. Sometimes what God used to get us through during the wilderness period in our lives is not what He intends us to have permanently. God supernaturally provided for us then, but now He wants us to learn to take our place of proper authority in the kingdom. God wants us to conquer and possess what is ours.

In the wilderness experience, Israel was journeying to the Promised Land. They finally came to a place where they had to act on the power of God's promise and come into their rightful possession. In order to motivate them to move into that place, God removed the "freebies" to make them get up and possess what was theirs. At various times in our lives, God removes the crutches and handicaps that we use as excuses for not wholeheartedly doing the will of God. We sometimes justify our existence in the wilderness for too long; therefore to ensure that we do not return, God cancels our benefits.

In order to become a possessor, we must have a renewed mind. All the great conquerors of the world conquered great territories. However, history has proven that most of them such as Alexander the Great, Genghis Khan, Napoleon, Stalin, Hitler, and even Great Britain upon whose empire the sun used to rise and set, lost the territories that they conquered. Why? I surmise that they did not learn how to possess what had come into their hands.

God did not tell Joshua to conquer the land, although we call their advance into the land the conquest of Canaan. God specifically told Joshua to "possess" the land. Why? The answer, I believe, can be found in the meaning of the word. The word "possess" translates from the Hebrew to mean "occupy by driving out the previous tenant and possessing in their place." It further implies to "seize and to inherit." This translation gives us much more than a good fight, but a mental attitude that what God has ordered for us is our divine destiny. (Maybe that will help you understand why our Hebrew brothers and sisters are so adamant about the land that God gave to our father Abraham. They divinely believe that it is their destiny to possess the land, and they are willing to die rather than compromise on God's promise.)

When we cross over and come into the revelation of our destiny, we must believe that what God has promised us is ours until the end. This is not a fatalistic attitude, but an undying, unyielding, and unbending faith in what God has said concerning our lives. It is this kind of faith that moves me to write these words to you. I just believe that this is a part of my destiny. When we get a vision from God for our lives, we must move toward its fulfillment no matter what.

Well, what else must we do now that we are over? The chapter of Joshua concludes with a manifestation of God's holy presence. An angel steps out of the invisible and becomes visible to Joshua. Joshua did not recognize this angel and inquired as to whose side the angel was sent to fight on. Apparently either Joshua did not remember the angel from previous experience under Moses' administration or had never seen this kind of angel before. The angel responds to his inquiry by identifying itself as being the Commander of the army of the Lord or what we would call an archangel. Isn't that amazing? Joshua did not recognize the angel.

Why did Joshua not recognize the angel? I surmise that they had wandered in the wilderness for so long that they lost sight of who they were really fighting against. They had warred against themselves for so long that the young leader Joshua did not understand the power available to him and the children of Israel to conquer their enemies.

Have you been fighting yourself for so long that when you get free and cross over you don't even recognize that God is on your side? Do you have trouble recognizing God when He releases His anointing on your behalf? That is what a long trip in the wilderness will do to you. It will make you forget why and what your purpose is all about. But rest assured that God is not coming to fight *against* you, but *for* you. This is your season and your time to move to the front and take—possess—what is rightfully yours.

Just as the angel had done in the burning bush with Moses over 40 years earlier, the angel now spoke to Joshua and told him to remove his shoes for he has come to a holy place. In that place, Joshua and the children of Israel came to worship the Lord in the beauty of His holiness. Wait a minute! That sounds familiar. Isn't worship the whole reason for getting the people out of bondage in the first place? Do you remember what Moses originally said to Pharaoh over 40 years earlier? He told Pharaoh to let God's people go so that they may go into the desert—three days journey—and worship Him. The whole premise for their release from bondage was to worship the Lord. Why worship? Because God knew that if they came to a mountain burning with fire and smoke and heard an audible voice declaring His will and purpose for their lives that they would not want to go back and be anyone's slave. How could they after witnessing the ten plagues, the opening of the Red Sea, and the safe passage to the mount of God?

Worship liberates your soul from the bondage of mediocrity and unfulfilled destiny. Worship frees the mind from the carnal concerns and earthly distractions that rob you of the fulfillment of your destiny. Worship elevates your spirit to full and perfect communion with your Creator. Worship restores your consecrated fellowship with God's divine presence and purpose for your life. Worship takes you back to your original purpose of being fruitful, having dominion, multiplying and replenishing the earth. Worship takes you out of the clutches of the adversary of your soul and transforms your thinking. Worship prepares you to conquer and possess God's destiny for your life.

After all these years, when you finally give God what He wants, you will find out that He will give you what you want. Right now, you ought to take a moment and enter into the most holy place to worship the one true and living God. You have access through the Blood of Christ. You have permission to enter through His Body. Come on in. He is waiting. Now that you're over what should you do? Worship!

Chapter 9

Designed To Win

When the trumpets sounded, the people shouted, and at the sound of the trumpet, when the people gave a loud shout, the wall collapsed; so every man charged straight in, and they took the city (Joshua 6:20 NIV).

Worship is the posture of the child of God. Constant adoration keeps our spirit in a receptive state to receive from God. Worship touches the heart of God and brings the move of God to us. The Hebrew translation for worship literally means to depress or prostrate oneself.

After we have been in worship, we are ready for conquest. We were designed for great victories through worship, which causes us to realize our position in relation to the Lord and promotes obedience to His commandments. When we forget how to worship, disobedience is not far behind. Disobedience stems from an unruly spirit which is not humbled by the worship experience. When we have been in true worship of the Lord, obedience is first nature and it is easy to follow what the Lord has commanded.

Worship precedes conquest, praise accompanies conquest, and thanksgiving follows conquest. This is the order when we move out from the presence of the Lord and in His power. It is just the opposite from when we enter His presence. When we come into His presence we "enter His gates with thanksgiving" then into His courts with praise. Then we prostrate ourselves as we enter the most holy place for worship, which is uninhibited adoration for who God is. After we worship— fall prostrate in the presence of God— we are ready to move out and conquer. While we are in the midst of conquering, we must continue to give God praise, for it is not by our might or power but by His Spirit that we are getting the victory. After we have won the battle and declared victory, we must return and give the Lord thanks for what He has done. Then the cycle begins all over again.

After Joshua had led the people in the memorial service and then worship, they were ready to conquer their foes. Worship had humbled their spirits to know that it is the greatness of God and not the goodness of man that would give them back their forfeited inheritance. With the right perspective in their relationship, the children were ready to take what was theirs.

The text in Joshua 6 opens up with the Israelite embargo against the city of Jericho. This embargo was not much different from the methods used by oppressed peoples everywhere. In the United States, African-Americans formed coalitions and engaged in strikes— embargoes— which brought down the citadels of injustice and social disparity. It was from the church where we worshiped that God gave us the victory as we marched, boycotted, and struggled for justice and equality.

Joshua and the children of Israel, had organized, formed a coalition, and forced an economic dilemma on Jericho. Their embargo (nothing in, nothing out) had wreaked havoc on the economy of the city. Indeed the walls were ready to come tumbling down because the city was in a desperate economic strait. More importantly, the city was theirs because worship had prepared them for the obedience necessary to overcome the enemy. In verse ten, Joshua gives the people the spiritual instructions that will bring them sure victory. "Do not give a war cry, do not raise your voices, do not say a word until the day I tell you to shout. Then shout!" Why the silent treatment?

In our warfare with the enemy of our souls, one of our greatest weapons is silence because the devil cannot discern our thoughts. He is not omniscient. The only way he can be successful against us is when we tell him what we are thinking and reveal our position. One of the reasons God gave to the Body of Christ the spiritual gift of speaking in tongues is so that we can have a coded language with God who can speak in our spirit and give us instructions without the devil being able to intercept and decipher the communications.

When the devil does not know what communications

have gone on between us and the Lord, he can only use the evidence of how he has known us to respond in the past. His database of information is filled with our old reactions, behaviors, and attitudes. When he fights us, he can only do so with old information. That is why it is important for us to understand that when we are in Christ, we have become a new creature; old things have passed away, all things are become new (2 Corinthians 5:17). It is through the act of worship that we are positioned to defeat the vulnerabilities of the enemy's network. The devil knows that our spirit is humbled and ready to obey the commandment of the Lord.

Can you imagine what the dwellers in Jericho were thinking when they saw the Israelites silently marching around their city? "What are these people doing? It seems strange." And so do the things that the Lord tells us to do. They seem strange to other people who cannot receive spiritual things nor discern them. God tells us to ask for something big and the natural man's wisdom tells him that it is impossible. Our goal is out of the question. What made Joshua and these wilderness wanderers think that they were going to just walk around a city for seven days and then the city would belong to them? It seemed so strange, but God's power and might was there to provide the victory.

On the seventh time around, when the priests sounded the trumpet blast, Joshua commanded the people, "Shout! For the LORD has given you the city! (Joshua 6:16)

Why shout? The shout is an announcement that something spectacular is about to happen. It makes those who were not expecting it to be filled with fear and those who were a part of it to experience a release in their lives. When we shout, our anxiety is released, and our anticipation is quenched. When Jesus returns, He will return with a shout. The world will be staggered by the noise, but the people of God will be released and caught up to meet Him in the air.

When the trumpets sounded and the people gave a loud shout in obedience to the Lord, the walls came tumbling down. The children of Israel were able to charge straight in because the Lord had given them the victory through their obedient worship.

You have been designed to worship the Lord! Worship! March! Shout! Charge straight in! You have been designed to win!

Chapter 10

Unfinished Business

Now Joshua was old, advanced in years. And the LORD said to him: "You are old, advanced in years, and there remains very much land yet to be possessed (Joshua 13:1 NKJ).

My father and mother always taught me to finish what I started before starting something else. This helped me to experience the satisfaction that comes with the completion of a task: the release of the burden and the joy of seeing my labor bring about a certain result. It is during this time that my work habit/work ethic was established. This discipline, though I did not always follow it, has helped me to see things through in life.

My mother's Saturday morning chore list would be taped to the headboard of our bed, the bathroom door, or even the bathroom mirror. These were three places I guess my mother figured I was sure to see. After the list of sweeping, scrubbing, and vacuuming, there would be a closing statement which read: "Have this finished by the time I get back."

I did not know it then, but it was this statement and others like it that shaped the attitude of success in my life. I did not know that when I struggled to choose between Bugs Bunny cartoons and chores, my mother was developing the conquering mind that I would need in my future.

The first lesson I learned from these disciplines of life (a.k.a. chores) was follow-through. Lack of follow through is what leaves a trail of incompletes or unfinished business in our lives. Many adults spend their time tying up loose ends from past inabilities to follow through. It is hard to live in the present and project for the future when you are still working on your past.

Many are still working on their past because they think that since the task is difficult, God must want them to do something else or go somewhere else. Many Christians are suffering from what I call the "The Lord is leading me" syndrome. Every time something gets difficult or challenges them to greater productivity, they quit, making the Lord their scapegoat.

The Lord did not lead them; they left because they were confronted with their own inadequacies, unfinished business, or incomplete tasks, and they did not want to humble themselves to get it right. Just because the way gets tough does not mean that God is not in something. Many times it is the Lord who has engineered the tough times to make us into what He would have us to be. Sometimes He wants to know if we will continue on the task assigned in spite of what is going on around us—what the leadership may say or do or the conditions we experience. Lack of follow through leaves some people stuck so far in the past that the present is gone before they get there, and the future is there before they arrive.

Another thing that I learned from these disciplines of life are the consequences of disobedience and the benefits of obedience. Proverbs 13:15 reads: "good understanding giveth favor: but the way of transgressors is hard." The time when life is most difficult for us is when we are out of line with life's guiding principles. That is why the study of the Word of God is so important. To know what the principles of life are, we must learn the ways of the Creator and Sustainer of life. We can't live by bread alone but we can have abundant life through the words that come out of God's mouth.

Obedience is not only an action, it is an attitude and if it is not in us, it will eventually be revealed. We can't fake obedience because it is founded on a spirit of submission. Submission is the mother of obedience. If we do not possess a submissive spirit, then we may look like we are doing what we are told to do, but it will soon be obvious that we really don't have an obedient spirit. Obedience is the oil that makes the wheels of life run smooth.

The other principle that I learned was respect for authority. The disciplines of life taught me to work and follow leadership. Conquerors must be able to follow leadership if they are to take what God has for them. As a pastor, I am not fooled by many people who will work with the pastor (although some won't even do that) but can't work under the leadership structure and chain of authority that God has ordered for the church. The writer of Hebrews records these admonishments for those who want to benefit from the disciplines of life: "Obey those who rule over you, and be submissive, for they watch out for your souls, as those who must give account. Let them do so with joy and not with grief, for that would be unprofitable for you" (Hebrews 13:17 NKJ). Respect for authority is an issue that challenges many. Throughout life we are accountable to and report to authority figures. In the church people may feel that they can "have it their way." That is far from the case.

One final thought which I learned was an appreciation for time. Everything works within the framework of God's timing. His purpose, which is eternal and knows no time limit, must be fulfilled in us within the parameters of time that He allots to us. We don't know how much time we have here on earth. We don't know how much time we have for the season that we are in right now. It behooves us to appreciate the time that God allows us and immediately move on the thing that He has told us to do. "To everything there is a season, and a time to every purpose under the heaven" (Ecclesiastes 3:1).

There were consequences for me and my sisters (of course, they had chores too) if we did not complete the assigned tasks when my mother returned. Yes, we had been left alone (my father was generally tending to some church matter). We had the choice of how we would use the time to follow through, obey, and hence show respect for authority. Needless to say, there were times when we did not value the time allotted, and it slipped away from us. My memory is slowing fading away from those moments, the corrections of life, which helped us to appreciate time in an entirely new way.

Joshua understood these disciplines of life and especially the importance of timing. He had come to know first hand how critical it was to the success of the Israelites in the present and for their future. He had lived through the rebellion of his contemporaries when, in disobedience, they refused to follow through with the Lord's direction to take the land. He had lived through 40 years of desert wandering while his generation (except for Caleb and himself) died out because of their doubt (sin) and unbelief. In the seeming sunset of his life, God acknowledged his age and challenged him to tend to the unfinished business of the conquest of the land. For God it was not too late, although Joshua may have had other thoughts.

You may be looking back right now and becoming discouraged by the things that you might have done differently. You may be looking forward and becoming discouraged by all of the things that you need to do now to impact your future for the better. There is nothing worse in life than coulda, shoulda, or woulda. You can't make up for lost time, but God can grace you to redeem the time. But you must be willing to move with Him now to regain whatever ground you lost or to possess what ground rightfully belonged to you. He is willing to help you. We need to tend to any unfinished business.

Chapter 11

More Than a Conqueror

*And now, behold, the LORD has kept me alive,
as He said, these forty-five years, ever since the
LORD spoke this word to Moses while Israel
wandered in the wilderness; and now, here I
am this day, eighty-five years old. "As yet I am
as strong this day as on the day that Moses sent
me; just as my strength was then, so now is my
strength for war, both for going out and for
coming in. "Now therefore, give me this mountain of which the LORD spoke in that day; for
you heard in that day how the Anakim were
there, and that the cities were great and fortified. It may be that the LORD will be with me,
and I shall be able to drive them out as the
LORD said (Joshua 14:10-12 NKJ)*

Have you ever been so battle worn and weary
that you don't think you have the strength to
conquer anything else? I have. But, then I look
at a man named Caleb and I am encouraged to go on.
For me Caleb is the epitome of a full and fulfilling life.
Although eighty-five years old, he was still alive and full

of energy to do the will of God. He was getting older, but he was not going to rust out. He was not going to retire, but he was going to re-fire. To me, Caleb is the quintessential character who defines what I am attempting to convey. He is old, but not tired of serving the Lord. He is battle worn, but not through with the fight. He is bruised and scarred, but not ready to quit. He is a conqueror and much more than a conqueror. He is a possessor!

Many times we have not taken the thing that God has set before us because we were not violent enough. We say we want it, but we don't have that "lean hungry look" that it takes to "GO FOR IT." We say we are sick and tired of the way things are going for us, but we are not sick enough nor tired enough to step up and out of our situation. We are not waiting on God; God is waiting on us to go after the thing that our lips keep saying that we want.

In Matthew 11, Jesus describes the faith that is inspired by the preaching of His cousin, John the Baptist. In verse 12, Jesus states the "kingdom of heaven is suffering violence and those who are violent take it by force." At first glance, you may assume that God's kingdom is in trouble. However, when you look at the definition of the words, you will find an amazing revelation about how to get from God what He is so willing to release to those who are passionate about their possession. The word violence literally translates "to crowd oneself into." The word violent translates "energetic." Well now. The Campbell paraphrase would read something like this: "Since brother John started preaching, God's people are coming alive with energetic faith. In the face of their energetic faith, God's kingdom gives permission for those who are passionate about their possession to push their way into its reservoirs of blessings. Those who do, get the stuff they are looking for." Are you coming alive with passion for pursuing your goals and dreams?

Wait a minute. I have another story about someone with a passion to possess the blessings of God. She is a woman who has been suffering with an issue for 12 years. Okay! I know the text says more specifically an issue of blood, but please allow me to take homiletic liberty in my exegesis. It does not matter what she was suffering with, her result was going to be the same. Whether it was an issue or an issue of blood, she had passion about possessing her healing. She was a conqueror and more than a conqueror. She was a possessor.

This woman, whose story is beautifully captured in Mark 5, gives us some wonderful insights about what passion for our possession can do for our situation. After suffering for 12 long years with her condition, she heard about Jesus' entourage passing through her side of town. The text does not say what she heard about Jesus, but whatever it was it was enough to ignite her faith to believe. Her next response was that she framed her faith. She set the condition by which she would receive her blessing. The way we frame our faith is the way our miracle will be built. After hearing and believing, she put her faith into action. She got up and moved toward her miracle. The result: She conquered her obstacles and came into possession of her blessing.

We need to develop the attitude of a good sales person:
- I am going in closing.
- If I am told "no" it is because I had to get the "no's" out of the way to get to the "yeses."
- There is no customer that I cannot sell to.
- Everything's for sale even if there is not a "for sale" sign in the window.

We need to activate our faith to begin to move toward the fulfillment of our goals and dreams. No more of this "I'm too old." "I am too young." "I was born at a disadvantage." "I don't have...".

The Apostle John says that "Beloved, I pray that you may prosper in all things and be in health, just as your soul prospers (3 John 1:2 NKJ). The word "prosper" means to "help on the road; to succeed in reaching; to succeed in business affairs." In order to prosper in something, we must be reaching for something to prosper in. When God sets before us a potential blessing, it is up to us to explore the potential that lies in it. Any blessings left unused or overlooked are not because God did not do His part. If we do not get what He has reserved for us, it is because we stopped short of our possession. We did not exhibit the violence or passion to get what had been reserved for us.

The other side to possessing is having the staying power to maintain what God has given to us. Many times you feel that God is supposed to just take over the day to day management of what He has given us. NO. NO. He has put the blessing into our hands and then it is up to us to take care of and prosper in the thing He has given us to do.

Now that He has delivered us from Egyptian rule, led us through our wilderness experience, and finally gotten us across our Jordan river, we must now possess the land. If we lose it, then it is our fault. God is not responsible for lost blessings. It is up to us to steward our blessings. As my mother would say, "I bought you the stuff, now you must keep up with it."

Now, if we do lose something or it was stolen from us, He may help us to recover it. When King David's wives and goods were stolen while he and his men were off in battle, the Lord did help them to pursuit, overtake, and recover everything (1 Samuel 30:8). The lesson for the next time is how to go out and do battle with the enemy and keep all our stuff safe while we are in the fight.

Possession is not just getting what we need but knowing how to keep it. That's why on many occasions after working great miracles Jesus said, "Go your way and sin no more." After the miracle came to change our lives, it is up to us to amend our lifestyles (change our ways) to maintain the miracle. The purpose of a miracle is to announce to us that God is desiring to do something new in our lives. The miracle changes our situation so that we may walk into a new lifestyle of blessings.

A pastor was sharing a story of one of his deacons who had suffered three heart attacks. After the first and second time, the pastor went to the hospital to pray for his healing. After the third heart attack, the pastor prayed: "Lord, keep deacon right here until he learns how to change his ways." The deacon's problem was not in believing God for a miracle, it was in having the faith to understand the change that the miracle brought about in his life. After each episode, the deacon would testify about God's miraculous healing power and then return to his same diet of pork and fried foods. He needed to know how to possess what the power of God had enabled him to conquer.

As the chapter closes with Joshua blessing Caleb to pursue his possession with passion, there is a wonderful summary to help us to move forward from this point. Caleb remembered God's promises to him and his past victories, which helped him to put his present into perspective. His assessment of the present was that he could certainly see God's promises fulfilled in his life in spite of his age. Why? Because it was God who made the promise. Finally, he rejoiced in the future that God had ordered for his life. He believed that the mountain that he was seeking would be his because God was with him. His conclusion—I can do this because I am more than a conqueror, I am a possessor.

Chapter 12

I Didn't Know I Had It in Me

Then the children of Joseph spoke to Joshua, saying, "Why have you given us only one lot and one share to inherit, since we are a great people, inasmuch as the LORD has blessed us until now?" So Joshua answered them, "If you are a great people, then go up to the forest country and clear a place for yourself there in the land of the Perizzites and the giants, since the mountains of Ephraim are too confined for you." But the children of Joseph said, "The mountain country is not enough for us; and all the Canaanites who dwell in the land of the valley have chariots of iron, both those who are of Beth Shean and its towns and those who are of the Valley of Jezreel." And Joshua spoke to the house of Joseph— to Ephraim and Manasseh— saying, "You are a great people and have great power; you shall not have only one lot, "but the mountain country shall be yours. Although it is wooded, you shall cut it down, and its farthest extent shall be yours; for you shall drive out the Canaanites, though they have iron chariots and are strong" (Joshua 17:14-18 NKJ)

Many times in life we are stretched and tested to new heights. This stretching experience is necessary for us to grow to new levels of experience. Without it, our lives would stand still and eventually we would be left behind.

Children are stretched to new heights as they go from child care to nursery to kindergarten and then on to grade school. Each new experience stretches them to a new level—a new dynamic—a new dimension in their life. As their life continues, moving from one level to another is marked by the celebration of graduation. From nursery to kindergarten we celebrate. From kindergarten to first grade we celebrate. From junior high to senior high there is a celebration. From high school—we celebrate. For those who go on to college, we continue the celebration of stretching when they graduate. For each level of stretching, there is a corresponding celebration.

There was a father that Jesus stretched to new spiritual heights. Jesus made the father reach deep within himself and come up with an honest confession. In Mark 9, Jesus came down from the Mount of Transfiguration to find a father whose son was possessed by a deaf and dumb spirit. While the boy was writhing on the ground, Jesus asked the father how long the boy had been this way. The father responded that it has been a long time. Then in verse 22 the father says something that triggers a spiritual breakthrough for both father and son. The father petitions Jesus, "If you can do anything to help us, please do so." "*If* you can?" Just as Joshua did with the children of Joseph, Jesus put the burden of proof back on the father. "If you can believe," said Jesus, "all things are possible to him that believes."

The father is stretched to a new point. His question has been answered by bringing the answer out of himself. The father cries out, "I believe, but there is some unbelief in me that needs Your help." The *honest answer* opens the door for new horizons of faith to be discovered. The father had made his unbelief evident by his question, "If you can." The implication was that there was a chance that Jesus might not be able to do something about the situation. Not only did Jesus deliver the boy, but he also freed his father from the doubt that had plagued him. Jesus stretched the man to new dimensions in his faith.

You may be going through a stretching experience like this father. God is stretching you to the outermost point of your faith. Why? Because He wants to increase your faith so that you can go to the next level of experience. God does not want you sitting, complacent in your Christian experience. He does not want you to remain at the level you are on.

Forgetfulness Leads to Complaining

Somewhere along the way, however, we can forget the stretching experience and become complacent. We can lose our elasticity and become resistant to the stretching that life puts on us. We may miss new opportunities and their benefits and blessings. If we become stagnant, content, and unwilling to move any further in life, we become complainers. We complain about going to work—doing a job that we do not like. We complain about our spouses in whom we find no more excitement and fulfillment. We complain about our children who we see as a burden rather than a blessing. We complain about our house, which is seemingly become too small to contain our family. We complain about our boss who seems to ask us to do more than we want to do although it is really not more than what our job entails. We complain about the food we eat, although the Big Mac is the same it has always been for the last 20 years.

We complain about our pastor whose message seems to challenge us to be more productive in our church and effective in our outreach. We complain about the church leadership who seems to be asking us to give more in the offering than we have ever given. Although we pay more for the food and clothes we buy, we are content to give God the same dollar we have been giving Him for years. We complain about the choir, who seems to be singing too many new songs, although the Lord said in His Word that we should "sing a new song" unto Him. We complain! We complain! We complain! But yet, the newness and vibrancy that would bring us true satisfaction—the joy that comes through productivity—lies within us all the while.

Most people only use about 10% of their God-given brain power. Just imagine if we were to increase that by 10%.

Our life would have 10% more satisfaction because we would be 10% busier tackling 10% more than what we thought we could do. We would discover untapped power that had been dormant in us all the while because we were not challenged to do any more than what we were presently doing. Imagine going out to play basketball with Michael Jordan. What would that do for our game? Imagine playing football with Emmett Smith. How about playing a round of golf with Tiger Woods? Would they serve as an inspiration to you? Would they force us to elevate our game?

Ask and You Shall Receive

The children of Joseph came to Joshua to inquire about the lack of size of their inheritance. Their request opened up a door of opportunity that they did not even expect. The response that Joshua gave them pointed them back to their own potential to possess the blessings of God. Their own complacency was revealed—it was the source of their internal dissatisfaction. Their needs were not met because they were not fulfilling their God-given destiny nor living up to their potential. This state is brought to bear in James 4:1-3.

Where do wars and fights come from among you? Do they not come from your desires for pleasure that war in your members? You lust and do not have. You murder and covet and cannot obtain. You fight and war. Yet you do not have because you do not ask. You ask and do not receive, because you ask amiss, that you may spend it on your pleasures.

Joshua helped them to focus on the source of the answer—their own untapped potential. Heaven will give us what we ask for.

> *Ask and you will receive. Seek and you will find. Knock and the door will be opened to you* (Matthew 7:7).

It is a principle. Asking humbles us, and like worship, it prepares us for the next level. Our answered request will bring us to a new level of understanding and thanksgiving. We are sitting in front of the door of blessing right now but many of us won't move toward it because the door is closed. A closed door does give the impression to most that it is also locked. Our door, however, is unlocked by the grace of God, and the blessing will open to us when we ask and then turn the knob.

Stop asking for less than what you really need and want from the Lord. Like the children of Joseph, you have been "devil whipped" into thinking that there is a limit to what God will do. Nonsense. The sky is the limit to what we can have. There is greatness within us that we have suppressed for too long. God wants to see us develop the fullness of the potential that He placed within us.

He wants us to be healed of our complacency and discontentment. He wants us to have a transfusion of faith to rid us of the doubt that is in our spiritual bloodstream, the doubt that keeps us from conquering and possessing what He has set aside just for us.

God knows that as long as we sit complaining about our condition, we will do just that—sit! We have to get up out of our seat of complacency to take what God has for us. Yes, He will be with us as we go, but in going we will discover that we had the greatness in us all the while to change our situation.

We will be stretched while we are reaching for that new goal—that new objective—that new target. We will certainly have to pay a price to take what is ours from those who temporarily are in control of it (notice I did not say they possessed it). We will have to fight for what is ours, but in the end, we will be satisfied when we realize the full potential of the greatness that God put inside of us. When we get to that point, we will realize that it is God that works in us to bring about what He wants for us. We will realize that we had it in us all the while.

Chapter 13

Don't Stop Now,
There's More To Come

*Now the whole congregation of the children of
Israel assembled together at Shiloh, and set up
the tabernacle of meeting there. And the land
was subdued before them. But there remained
among the children of Israel seven tribes which
had not yet received their inheritance. Then
Joshua said to the children of Israel: "How long
will you neglect to go and possess the land
which the LORD God of your fathers has given
you?* (Joshua 18:1-3 NKJ)

Sometimes we feel that when we have done something new, gone somewhere different, or seen something new; that the experience of doing, going, seeing is enough in and of itself. No. There is a greater reason than what we may presently see for the Lord stretching us to a new place in Him. Our miracle is not just for us—but it is for us to share with others so that they too may come to know God's goodness in their lives. Our blessing was not just for us, but for us to be an example to others of the goodness of God. Yes, He is personally concerned about us, but we must also be aware that His purpose not only includes us and our needs but the countless hundreds or even thousands with whom we come in contact.

When we do not do—or possess—all that we are supposed to, someone else will relax in their comfort zone, thinking that it is alright for them to stay just where they are too. Children will only go as far as parents go. That is why parents should always encourage their children to seek information and direction from those who may have gone farther in their lives than they have. It is alright, we will not lose our children, as a matter of fact, they will appreciate us more for pointing them in the right direction although we may not have attained that goal ourselves. Many of our parents and grandparents struggled to make better opportunities available to us than what they themselves were able to enjoy. Because of their sacrifice, we must do more than what we are presently doing—our accomplishment is a testimony—a reward for their effort. We can't sit back and relax just because we have a nine-to-five job, a nice home, pension, or paid vacation. We must strive to do for others around us. When we move into our inheritance, they will be inspired to possess theirs too.

As soon as we get through rejoicing over our great conquests and victories that the Lord has given to us, we must still have that "lean, hungry look" that it takes for us to maintain—possess—our blessing. We can't forget that there is a blessing when we are hungering and thirsting after God. Many people have laid back after great accomplishments only to fall asleep on the greatness of their past. Wake up! Each day is an opportunity to push a little further in our conquest. Each day is an opportunity to share with others what we possess, knowing that by sharing, we position ourselves to be blessed even more.

People are inspired by what God has done in the past. The joy of hearing His miracles and blessings does encourage those who hear. People not only want to hear what happened yesterday, they want to know what God is doing today. When we are "in motion," we testify that He is indeed the same "yesterday, today and forever," and that He is ready right now to work a miracle.

In Joshua 18, we see that there were those who had not received their inheritance. It was not because it was not for them, it was because they had not gone up to possess what was theirs. They were not waiting on God, but He was waiting to show Himself strong in their lives when they moved.

The door is open but we shouldn't get comfortable with just a portion of what is ours. We must have the mindset that "I cannot rest—I cannot be slack—until I have come to possess all that He has for me. My life depends upon it—the lives of my children depend upon it. I must overcome all my enemies while the anointing is upon me to conquer and possess." We must know when it is our day—when it is our time to shine. We only have so much time given to us on the stage of life. If we don't move at that time, some things that we were destined for will be lost forever. God will grant us His grace, but some things we will forfeit if we don't have the right response at the right time.

Look back at the generation before Joshua. Moses, one of the greatest prophets who ever lived, led the children of Israel—God's chosen people—to the border of their blessing. They actually stood on the banks of the Jordan. God was ready for them to go in and possess what was rightfully theirs. So what happened? They did not recognize that is was their time to be blessed. They hesitated and did not move toward the thing that God had ordered for them. Their lack of faith caused them to miss out on so much that they could have had.

Was God angry? He was more disappointed that the people He had "designed to win" did not believe in Him and also in themselves. He was grieved that because of their fears, habits and ignorance, they were refusing what He had prepared for them. "But they rebelled, and vexed his holy Spirit: therefore he was turned to be their enemy, and he fought against them" (Isaiah 63:10). God was feeling not much unlike the mother who has prepared dinner for her children only to be told "I'm not hungry—I don't want any." After they hesitated, God is still who He is. Not moving into their possession did not take anything away from Him. When we do not possess what He has designed for us, He does not lose anything.

81

It is we who lose out on the opportunity to change our future and that of our children.

After conquest there is a tendency to become satisfied. We should be delighted with what the Lord has wrought through our hands. But we must remember there is always more to the Lord and His purpose than we will ever come to know in this world. He has much more for us than what we have already conquered and possessed.

Get up and get in motion. Don't be slack—faint—still—abated. Get up and possess the land, drive the devil out of tenancy and control your blessing. Don't you give out! Don't you give up! Don't you give in! Whatever you do, don't stop now; there is so much more to come.

Chapter 14

Keep Me in Mind

I have given you a land for which you did not labor, and cities which you did not build, and you dwell in them; you eat of the vineyards and olive groves which you did not plant. Now therefore, fear the LORD, serve Him in sincerity and in truth, and put away the gods which your fathers served on the other side of the River and in Egypt. Serve the LORD! And if it seems evil to you to serve the LORD, choose for yourselves this day whom you will serve, whether the gods which your fathers served that were on the other side of the River, or the gods of the Amorites, in whose land you dwell. But as for me and my house, we will serve the LORD (Joshua 24:13-15 NKJ).

When God has purposed to bless us, nothing can stop the blessing from coming upon us, but we ourselves. We can delay God's blessing for our lives by our responses. We can provoke God with our actions, and He will revoke His plans as He did with the children of Israel when Moses brought them to the

Jordan river the first time. However, if our response is favorable, once His promise has gone out of His mouth, that's it. We might as well get ready to be blessed.

In the process of coming into our blessing, there is a testing that we must go through. God wants to see if we have it in our heart to continue on with Him after He has blessed us.

Many times in our relationships we have tested the resolve of someone by giving them something of value to us. This was a test to see if they would continue in the relationship or move on to something or someone else. Many times we have been deceived and our heart has been broken when they did not value us or our gift as we thought they should.

Serving the Lord With Gladness

God brings us through our experiences to deliver into our hands the thing that He has promised to us. Resting in our hands, however, is the power to maintain His blessing and to sustain our commitment to Him. That is what possession is all about. After all that the Lord has brought us through, we should be willing to serve Him with all of our heart.

Solomon helps us to summarize a life of devotion to God. Let us hear the conclusion of the whole matter: "Fear God, and keep his commandments: for this is the whole duty of man" (Ecclesiastes 12:13 KJV). Our purpose for being here in the earth is to bring praise and glory to God. For that purpose to be perfected, God arranges our lives so that His praise can be continually in our mouth. He blesses, works miracles, prospers, heals, saves, delivers, and answers our prayers so that we may return to Him the praise He deserves. When He does all of these things for us, it stands to reason that we should be willing to give Him what He is asking for. After all the things He has done for us to make us happy, is it too much to give back to Him what will make Him happy—praise? We should be willing to give Him praise—it is His possession. It belongs to Him. We should be willing to give Him anything and everything that we have.

We should be willing to give Him our *treasure* (nice word for money). Not just our money, but the top tenth—tithe—of everything that He blesses us with. The tithe—which is really the Lord's and not ours anyway—is an expression of our devotion. I define giving as the "outward expression of the inward appreciation for what the Lord has done for us." God so loved that He gave. He gave us everything that we need to live an abundant life. By bringing the tithe to the Lord, we are letting God know that He is in the forefront of our thoughts.

We should be willing to give Him our *time*. He took the time to chart our lives in the pathway of blessings, so we should be willing to arrange our time to include His desires in our schedule. If we delight ourselves in Him, He will in turn give us the desires of our heart. It is not just enough to bring Him our treasure (possessions)—we must also give Him ourselves. Our treasure comes from Him anyway so we would just be giving Him what He already owns. When we give ourselves, we are giving Him the highest expression of His creation. We are making a conscious decision to worship and love Him. Now that is a gift.

We should be willing to give Him our *talent*. Our talents are the skills that He has blessed us with. Our talents are the natural enablements and resources at our disposal. Our talents—when used to His glory—express His presence in the earth. When we make our talents available to God, we are letting Him know that we appreciate what He has entrusted us with.

Another way to keep God in mind is by remembering to help minister to other members of the household of faith. One of the attributes of God is that He is not forgetful. "For God is not unrighteous to forget your work and labor of love..." (Hebrews 6:10 KJV). The writer of Hebrews draws a correlation between unrighteousness and forgetfulness. I know that we say that it is human to forget, but that is just it: it's human (fleshly). When we forget to show kindness and to minister to the household of faith, it is unrighteous. Show righteousness and do good to the saints. If we want God to remember us and keep us in mind when He is passing out blessings, then we need to keep Him in mind when the opportunity comes to bless someone else.

In the closing chapter of the book, Joshua reminds the

people of how far the Lord has brought them. He takes
them all the way back to Terah, the father of Abraham.
In doing so, He reminds them of their humble begin-
nings. They were not always walking in the righteousness of God. His closing sermon to the Israelites brings
them from their slavery sojourn in Egypt to their wilderness experience. He reminds them of the crossing of the
Jordan river and the power of God that has brought
them into possessing what they now have. He brings
them all the way to their present and encourages them
not to return to the past practices of idol worship.

Sometimes, we too need to reflect on where the Lord
has brought us from. There may be times of pain and
suffering that may be difficult to revisit. But that is our
history. It is good to keep our history in mind. It helps to
keep us humble by reminding us of our need for the
Lord. Where is the glory in our story? The glory is in
God whose mighty hand has redeemed us from the
bondage of our history and empowered us to turn our
pain into power. There is a little song which helps to always call to remembrance the blessing of God in our
lives:

Jesus, I'll never forget what you've done for me.
Jesus, I'll never forget how you set me free.
Jesus, I'll never forget, how You brought me out.
NO, NO, NO, NO, NO, NEVER!

Joshua made a final plea in his message for the people to
serve the Lord, and they responded with "Amen." After

that he invited them to renew their covenant with the Lord and set aside a stone which is a witness of the renewal. After this final message, he recorded the events of that day along with their history of conquest under his administration. At the age of 110 years, Joshua died. He had fulfilled his destiny of bringing the children of Israel into their possession. What a satisfying life. What a fitting conclusion to the exodus/conquest period in the history of the children of Israel.

What will your story record after you are gone? Will you have served the Lord and fulfilled your destiny? Will the record show that you conquered the obstacles in your life? Will it show that you were more than a conqueror? Will you be a possessor of all that God has ordained for your life? I hope so. I encourage you to be a conqueror and much more than a conqueror. I want you to be a possessor. Go ahead! Conquer and possess!

Special Remembrance

Subsequent to the release of this book, my personal mentor and a lifelong friend of my father and mother— Reverend Dr. Henry A. Hildebrand—went home to receive his eternal reward. Pastor Hildebrand was one of the members of the board of my ministry and a trusted advisor and confidante. His wisdom guided me through many critical times in my life and ministry.

The first chapter of this book, entitled "Leave the Past Behind," was preached at his last assigned church— Mount Zion African Methodist Episcopal Church in New Brunswick, New Jersey. There, under his leadership, I was privileged to preach many revivals and services. At first I was grieved that he did not have a chance to read this work, but through the assurance of the Holy Spirit, I was encouraged to share this special dedication to his memory.

Dr. Hildebrand was a man of integrity and excellence who left us all a road map to follow. Now, he and my late father—Reverend W. Melvin Campbell, Sr.—are together again, rejoicing in the presence of our Lord and Savior, Jesus the Christ. Servant of God, well done!

To contact the author for speaking engagements:

Reverend William M. Campbell, Jr.
Flaming Fire Ministries
P.O. Box 10776
Killeen, TX 76547-0776
website: www.flamingfire21.org

Other works by Rev. Campbell:
Born to Dream